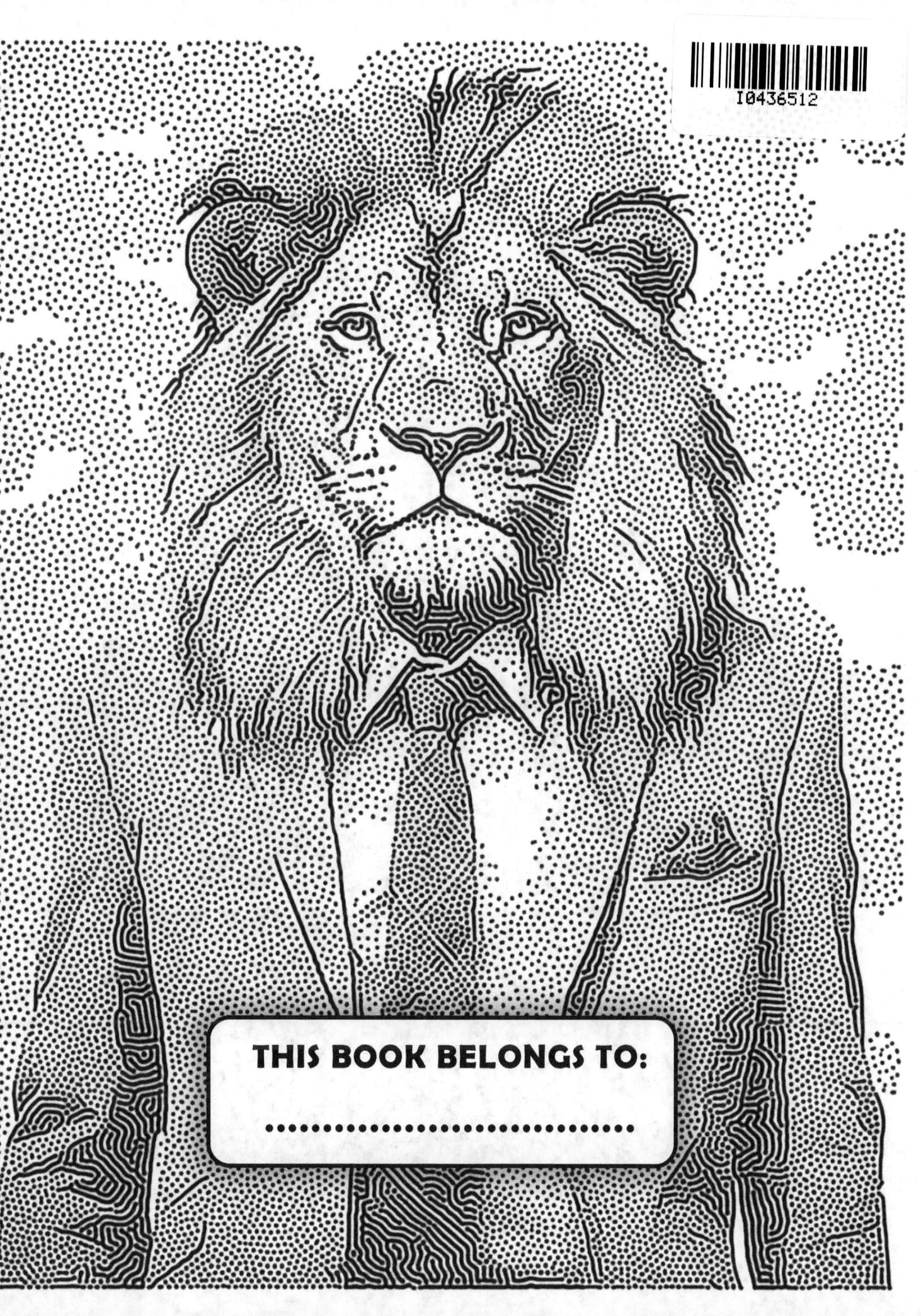

THIS BOOK BELONGS TO:

....

THANK YOU FOR CHOOSING US
TRY OUR OTHER COLORING BOOKS ON AMAZON

- Lily Ann Coloring Book -

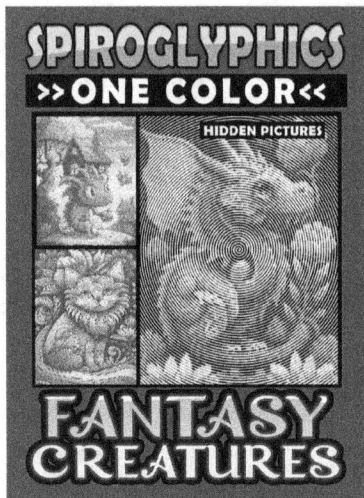

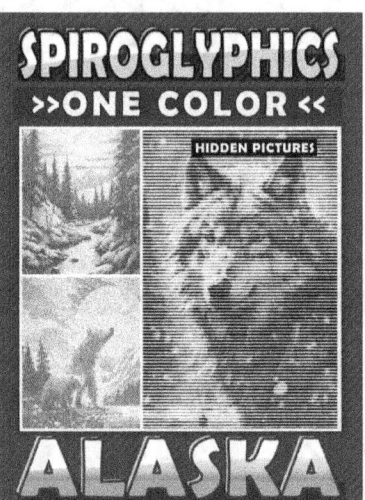

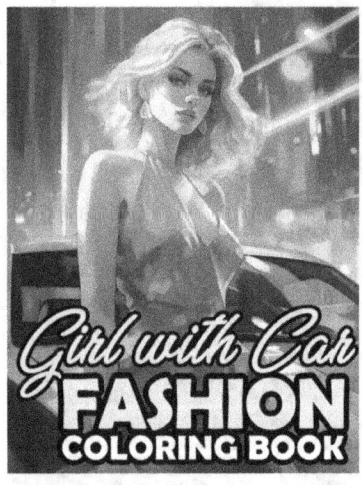

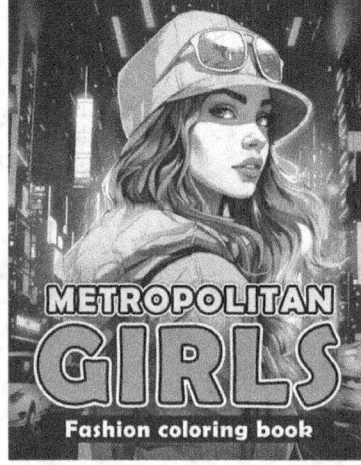

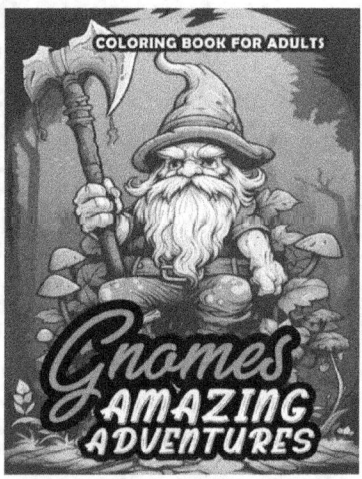

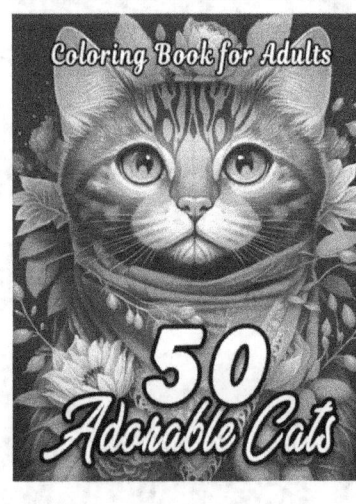

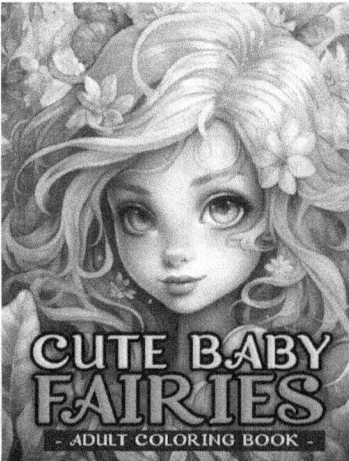

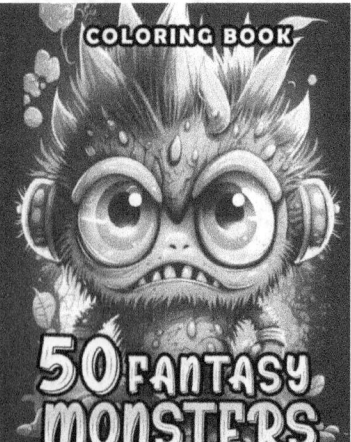

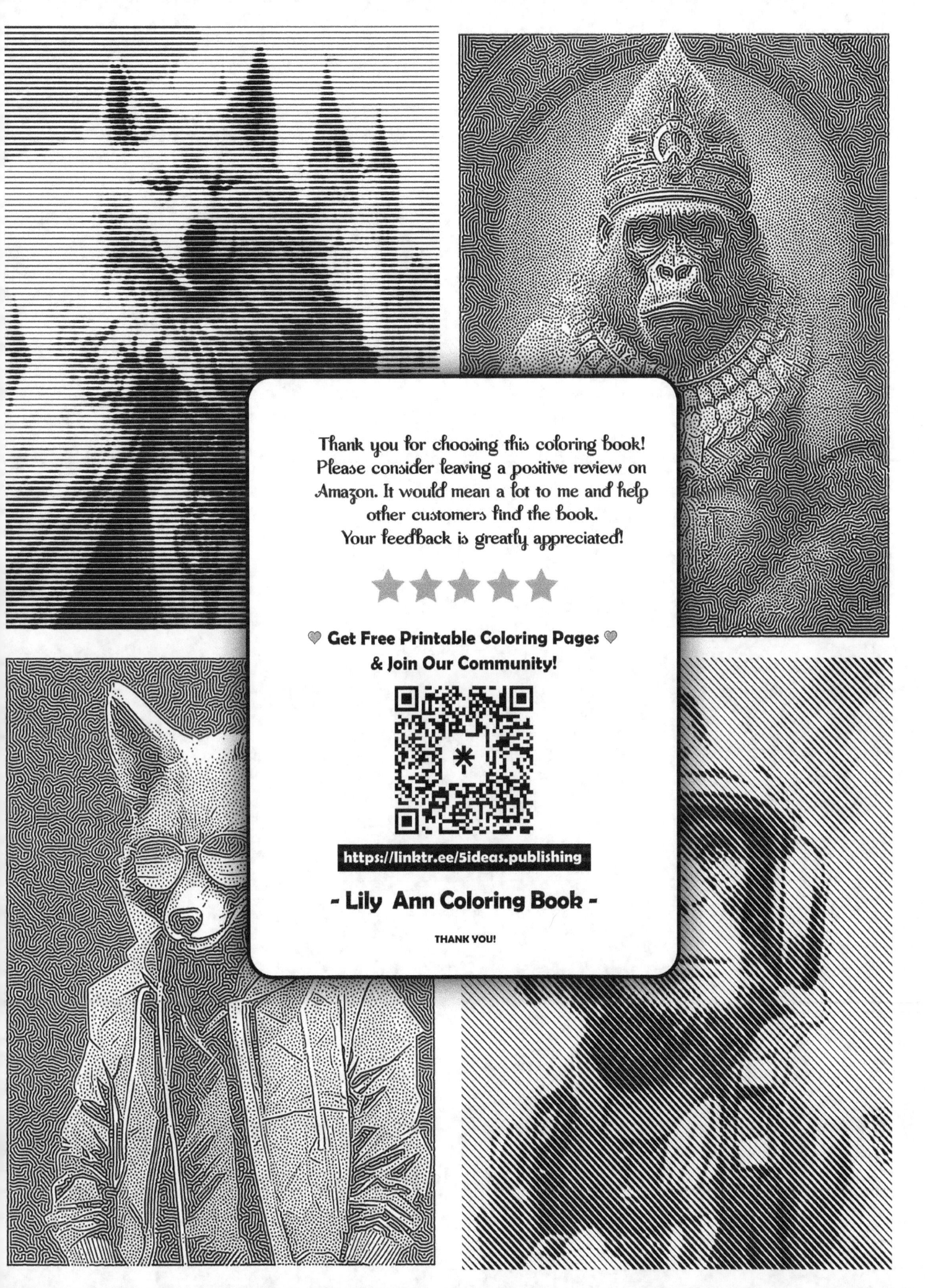

Thank you for choosing this coloring book!
Please consider leaving a positive review on
Amazon. It would mean a lot to me and help
other customers find the book.
Your feedback is greatly appreciated!

★★★★★

♡ **Get Free Printable Coloring Pages** ♡
& Join Our Community!

https://linktr.ee/5ideas.publishing

- Lily Ann Coloring Book -

THANK YOU!

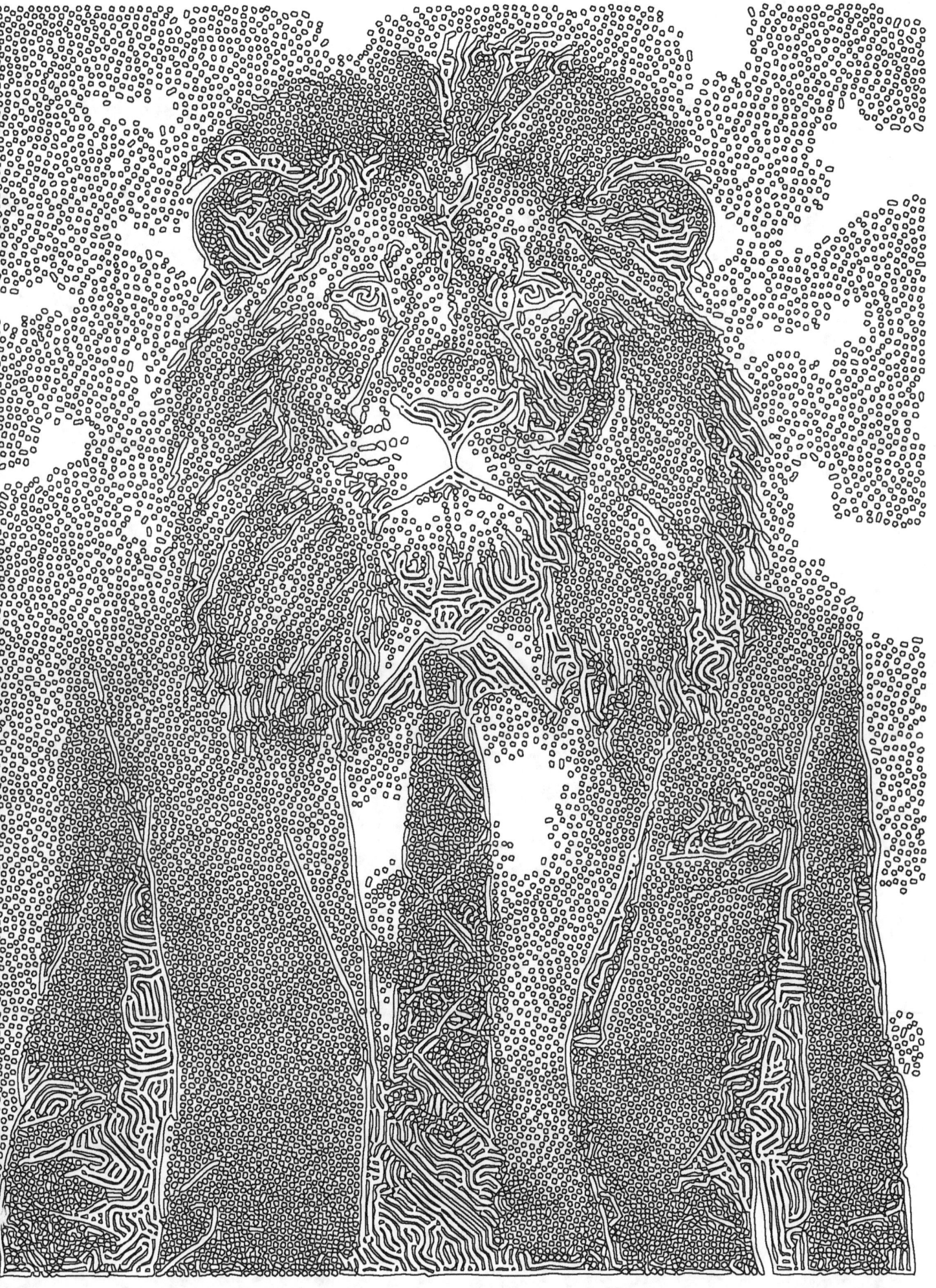

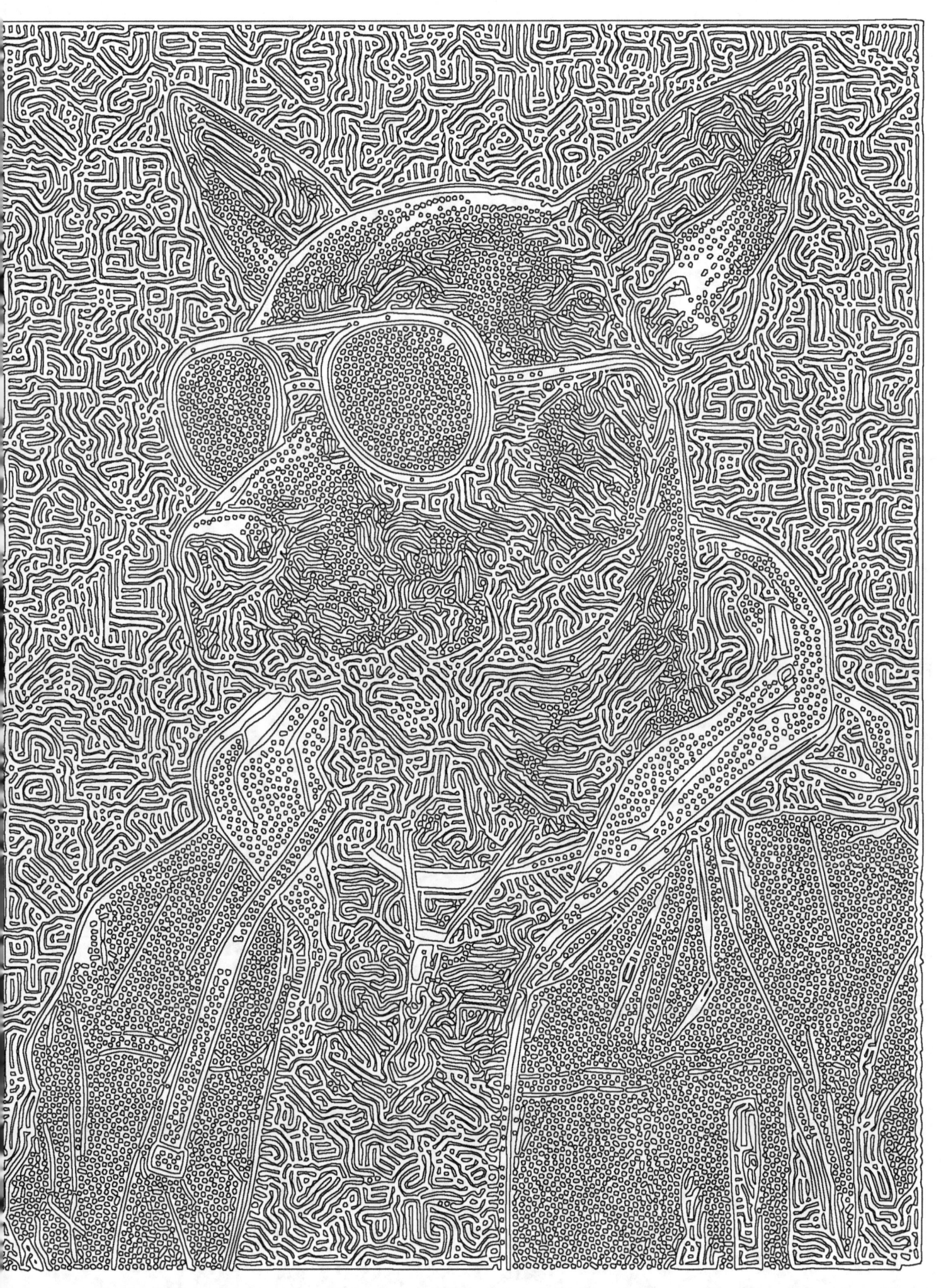

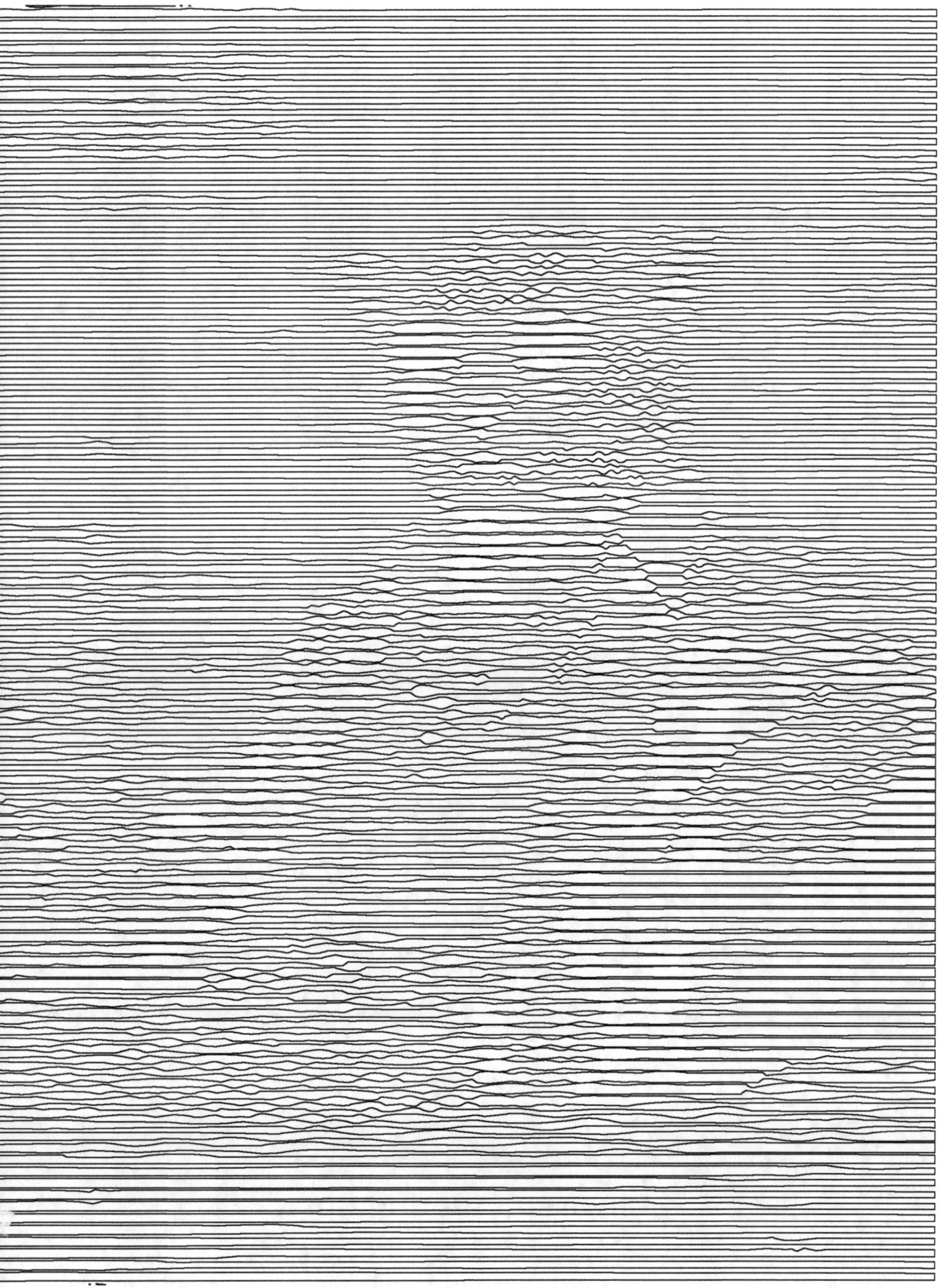

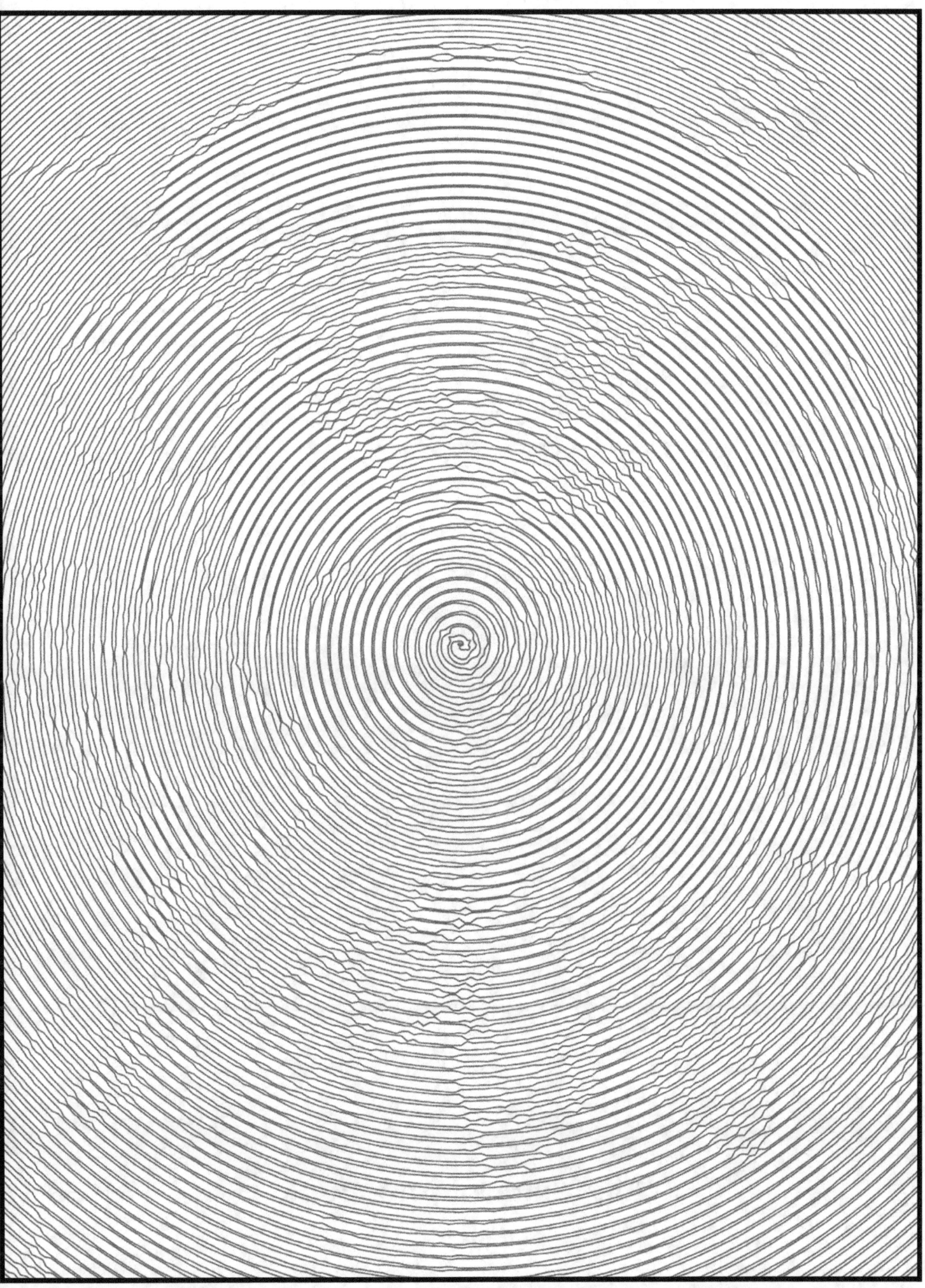

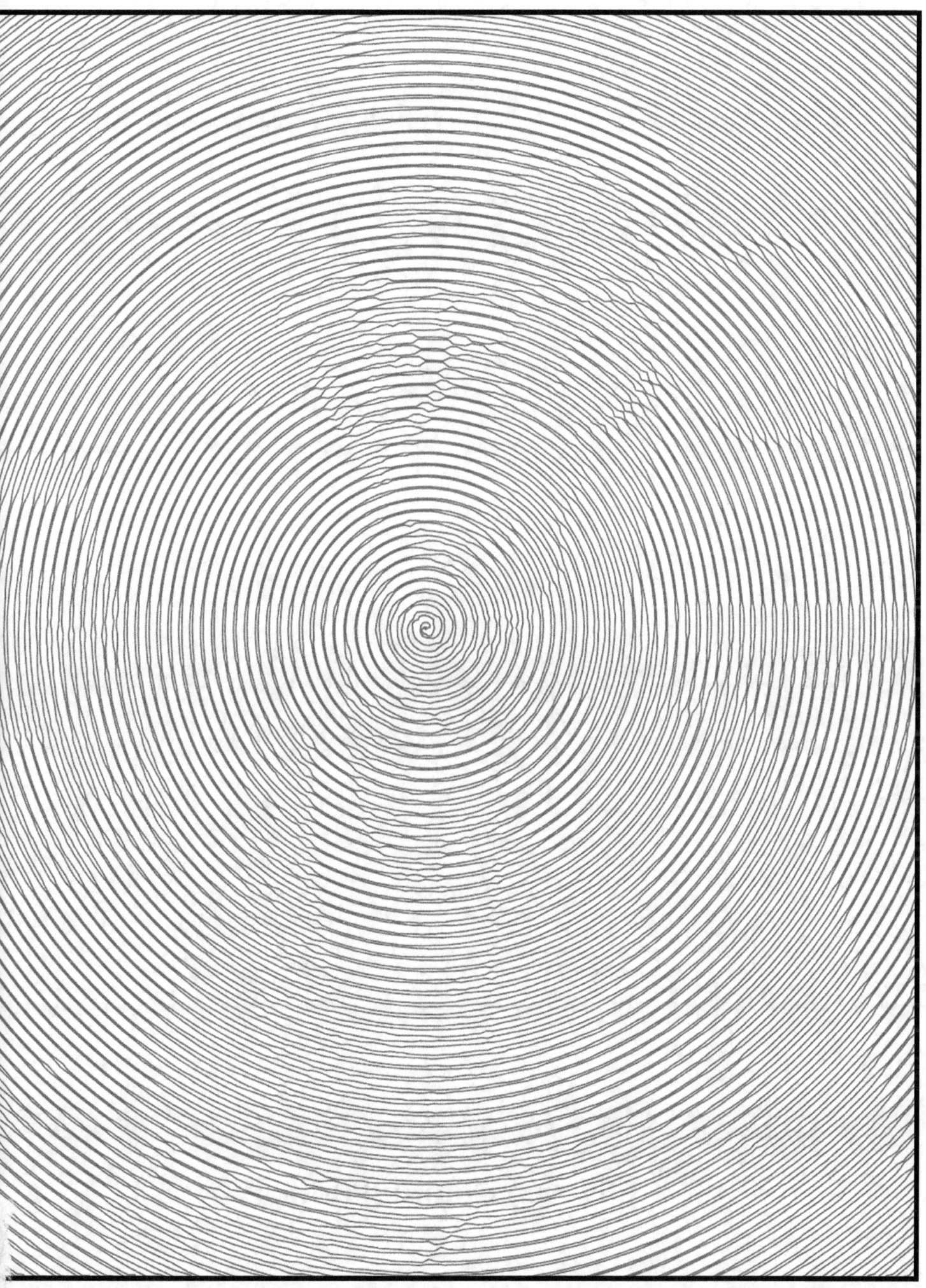

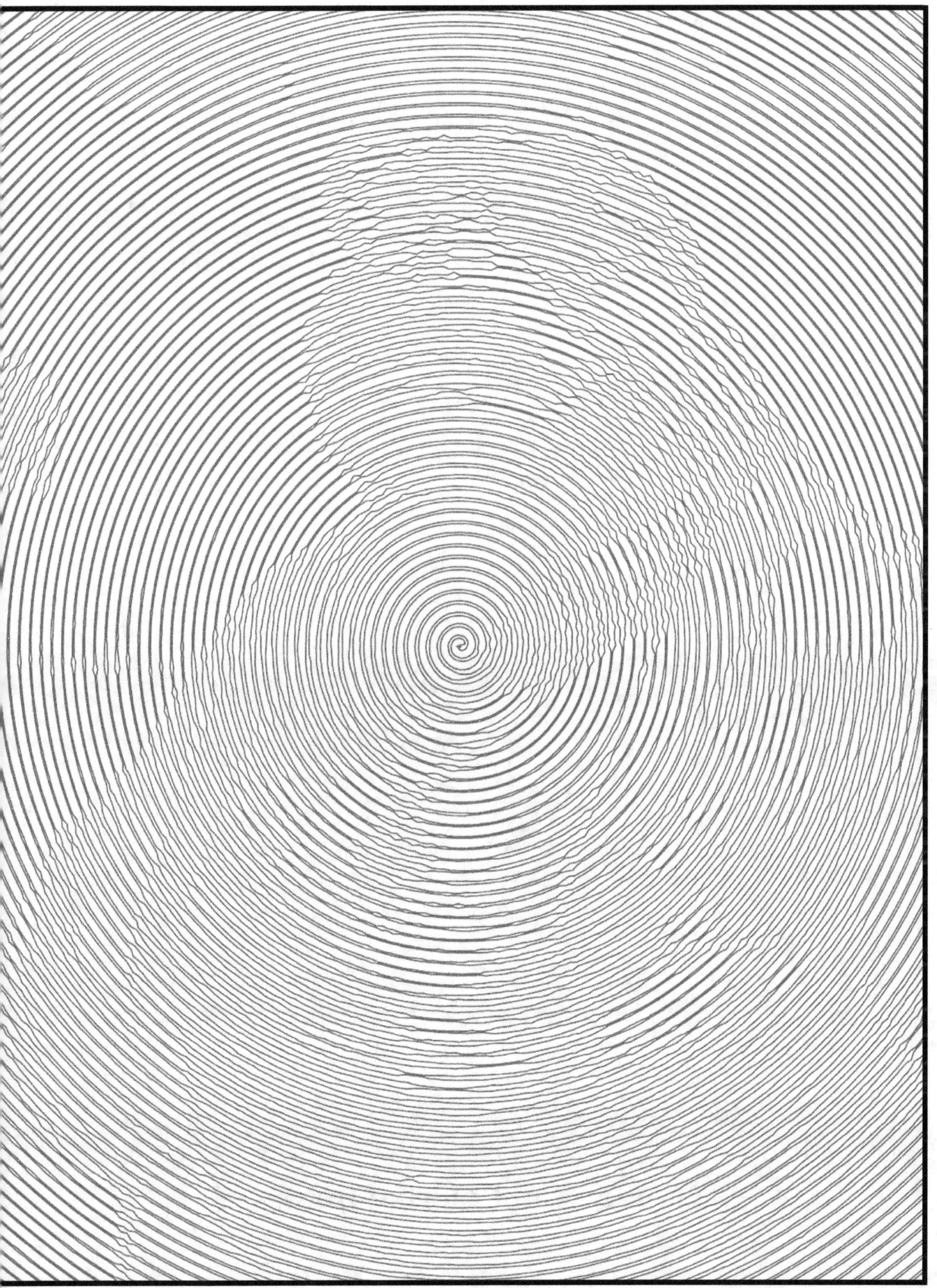

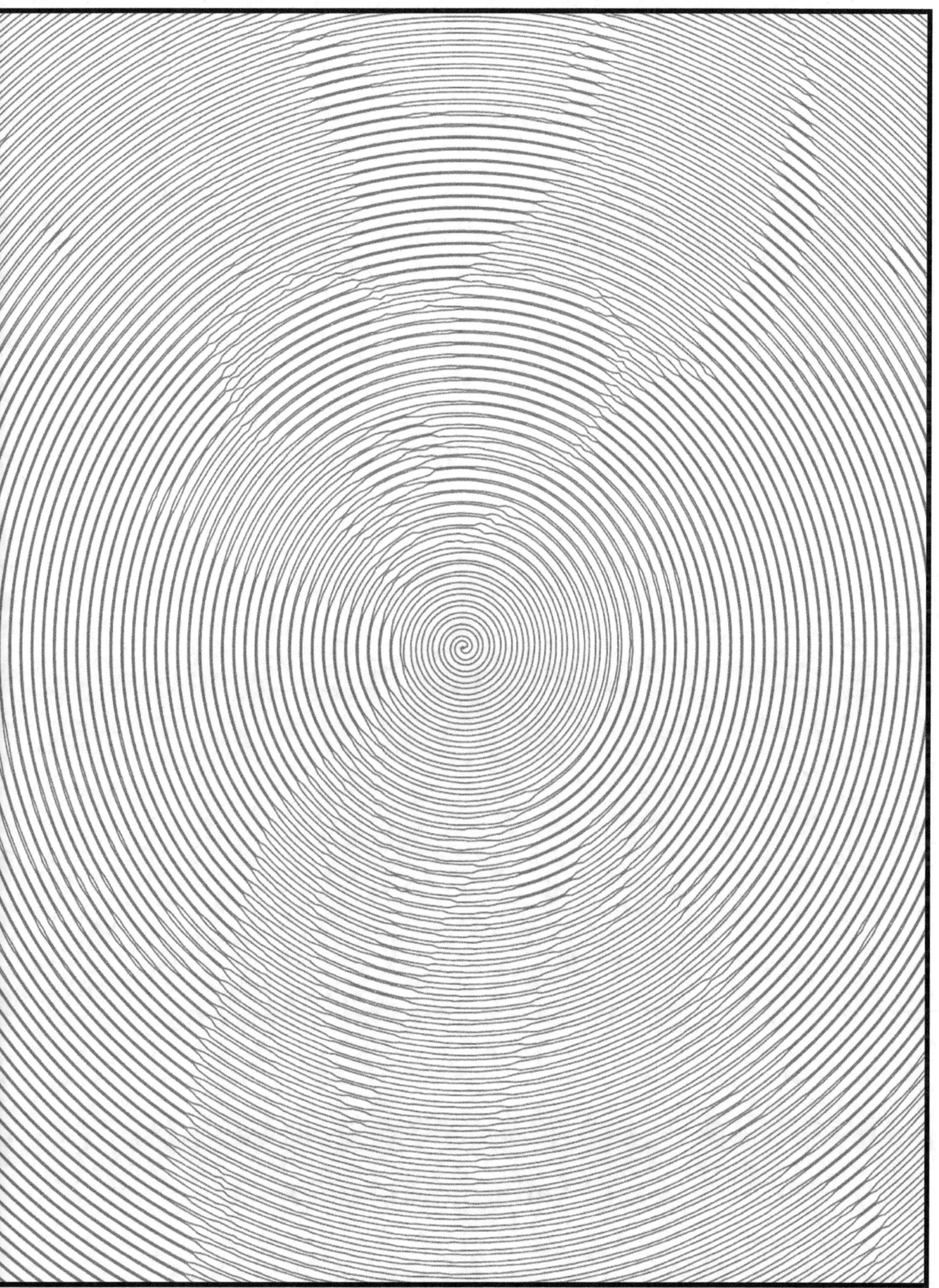

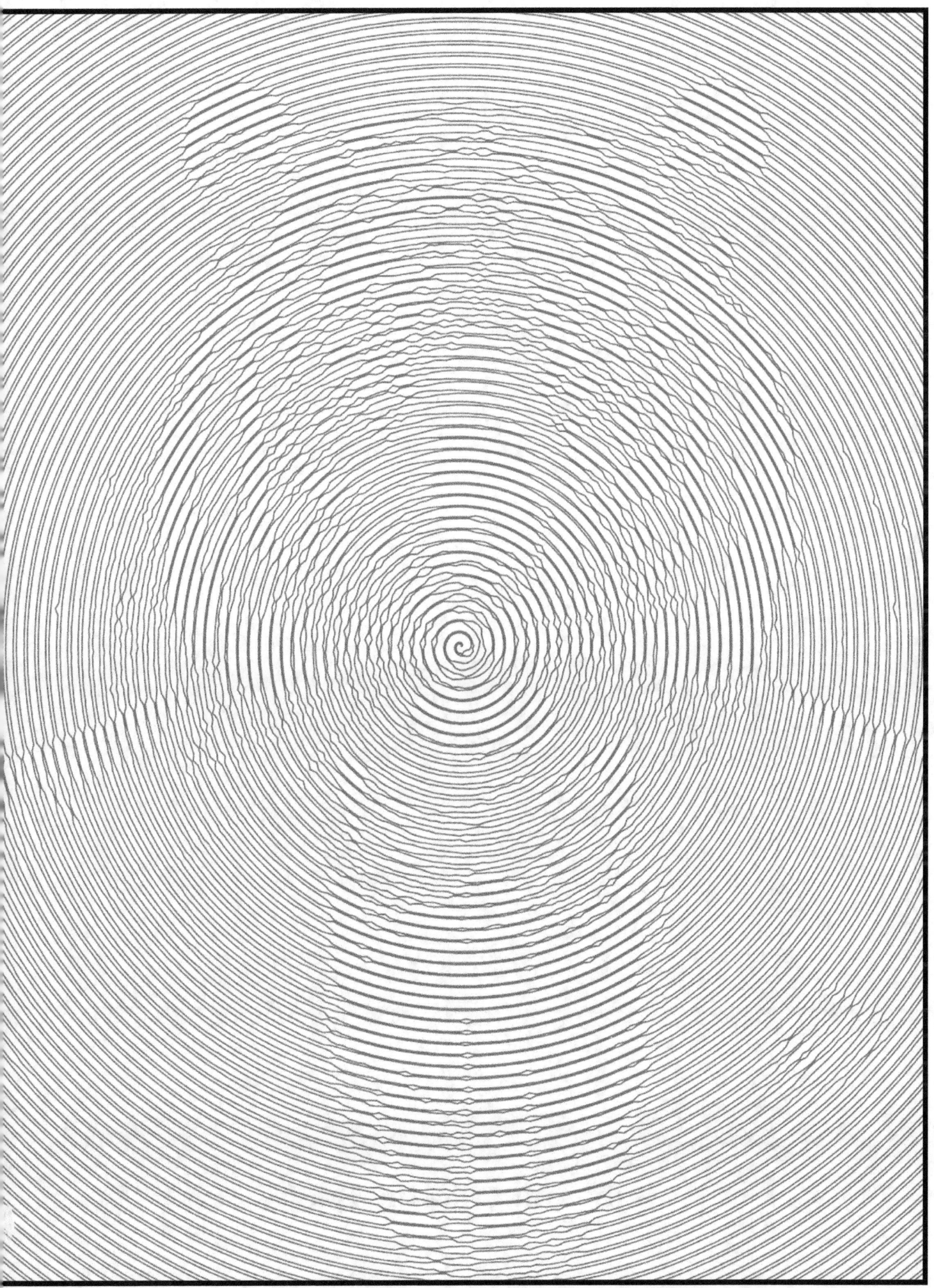

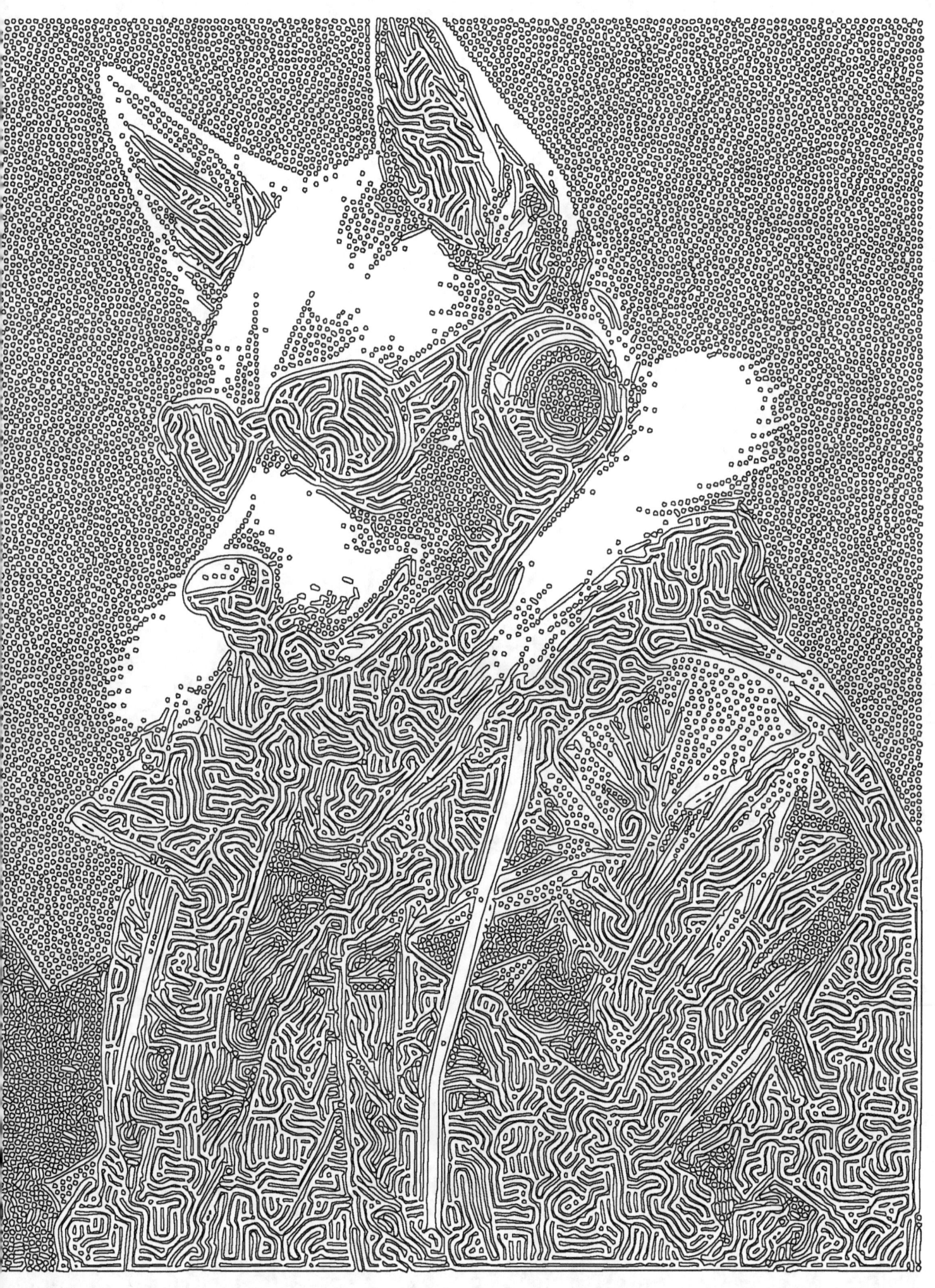

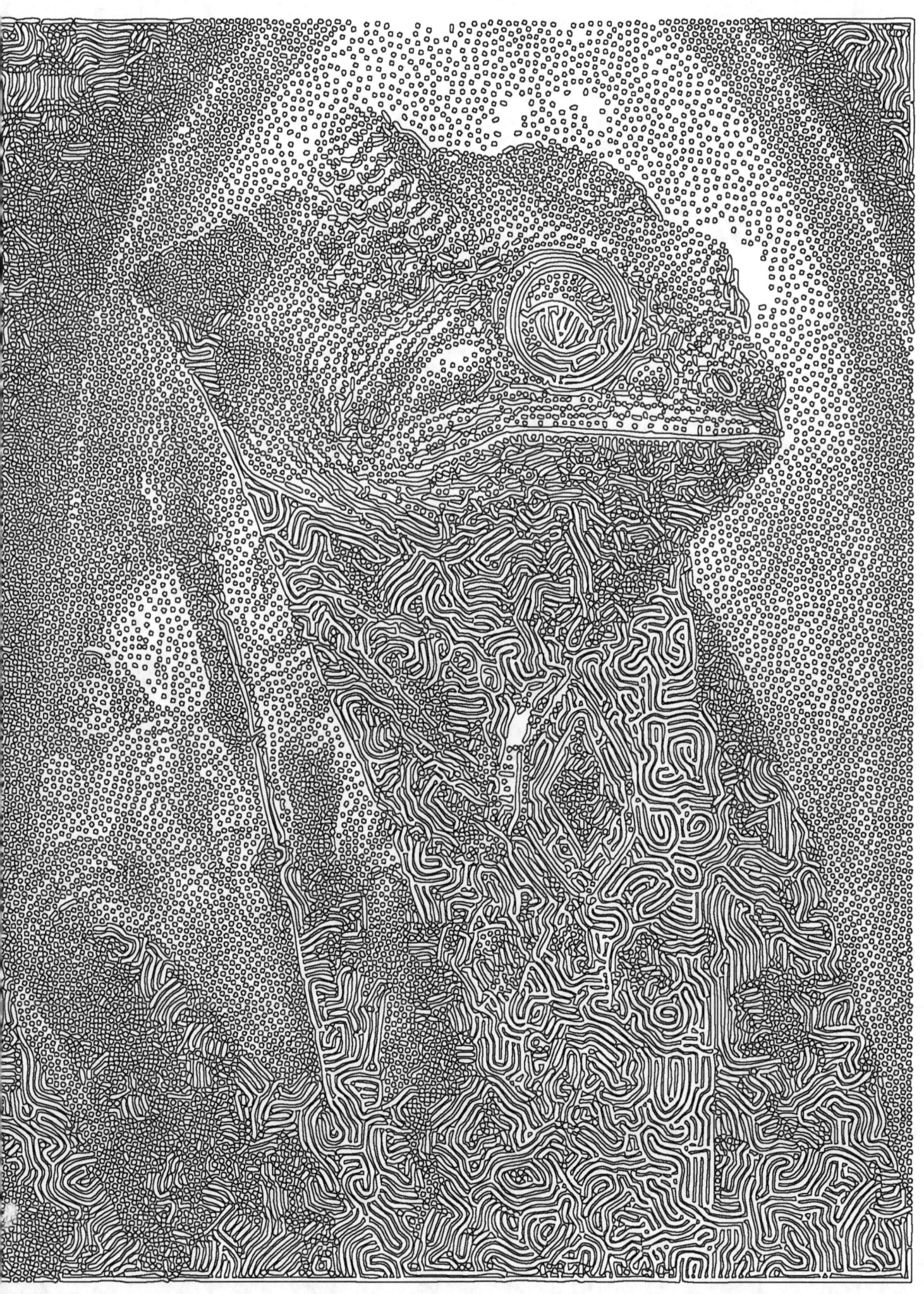

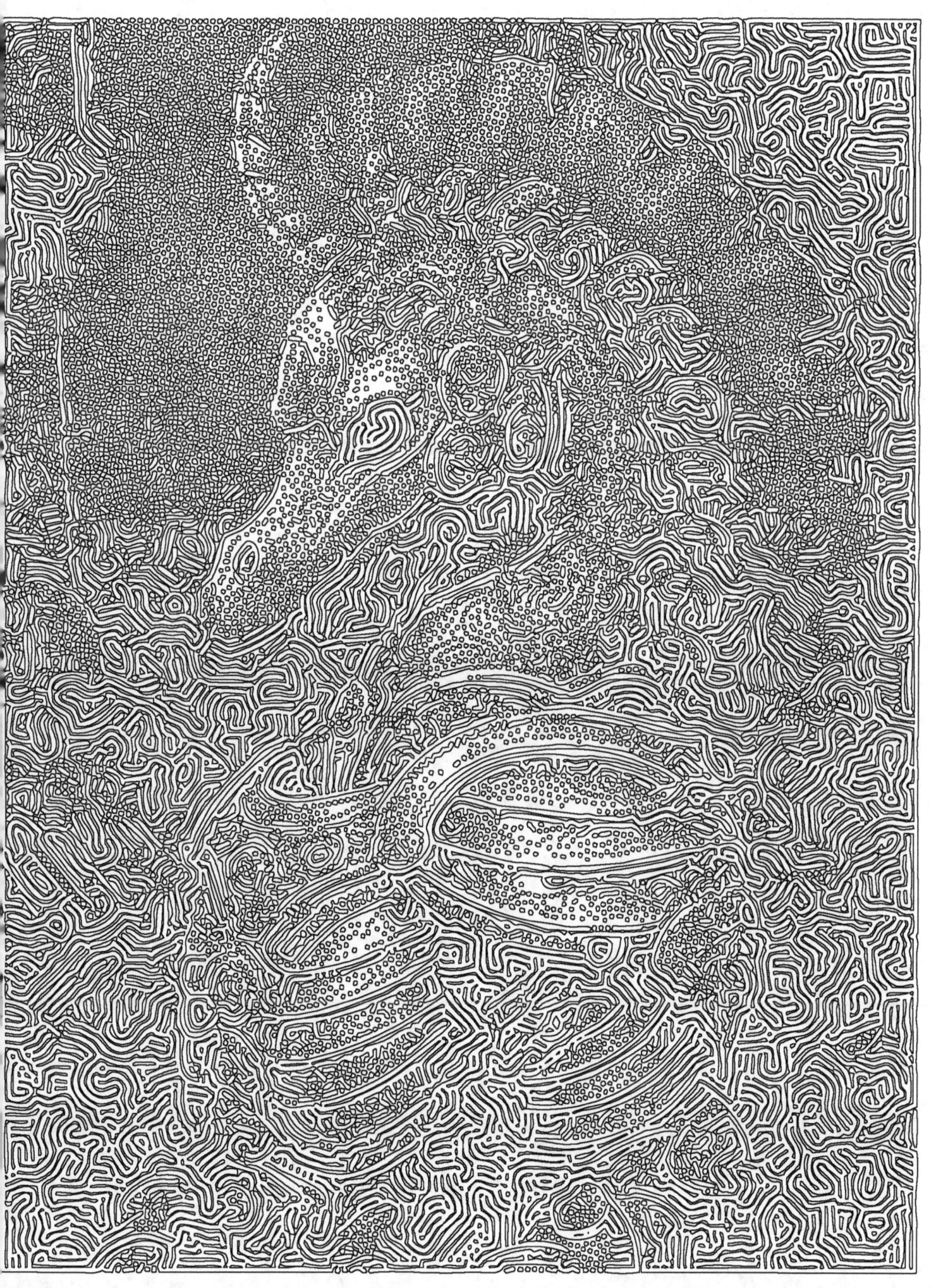

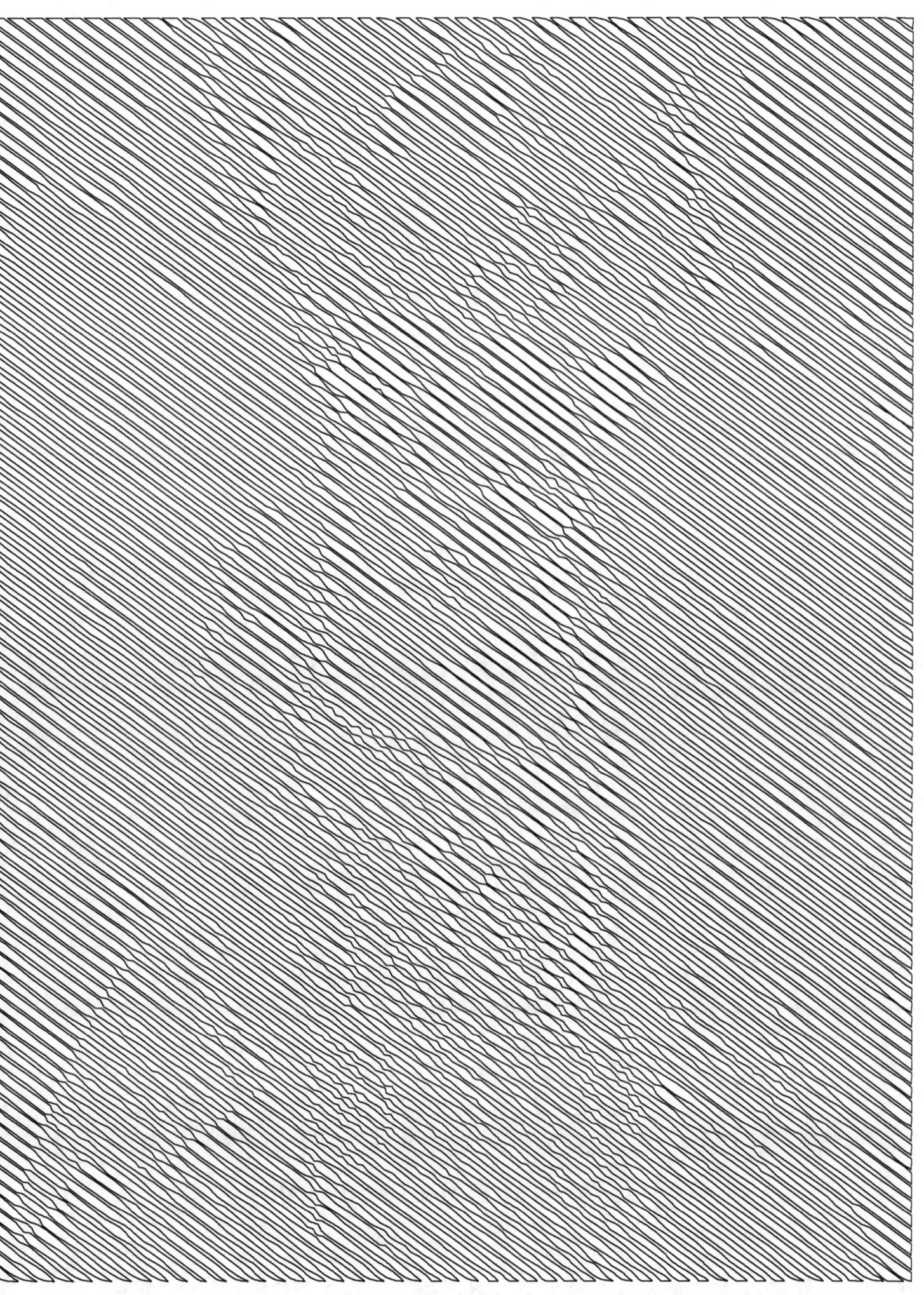

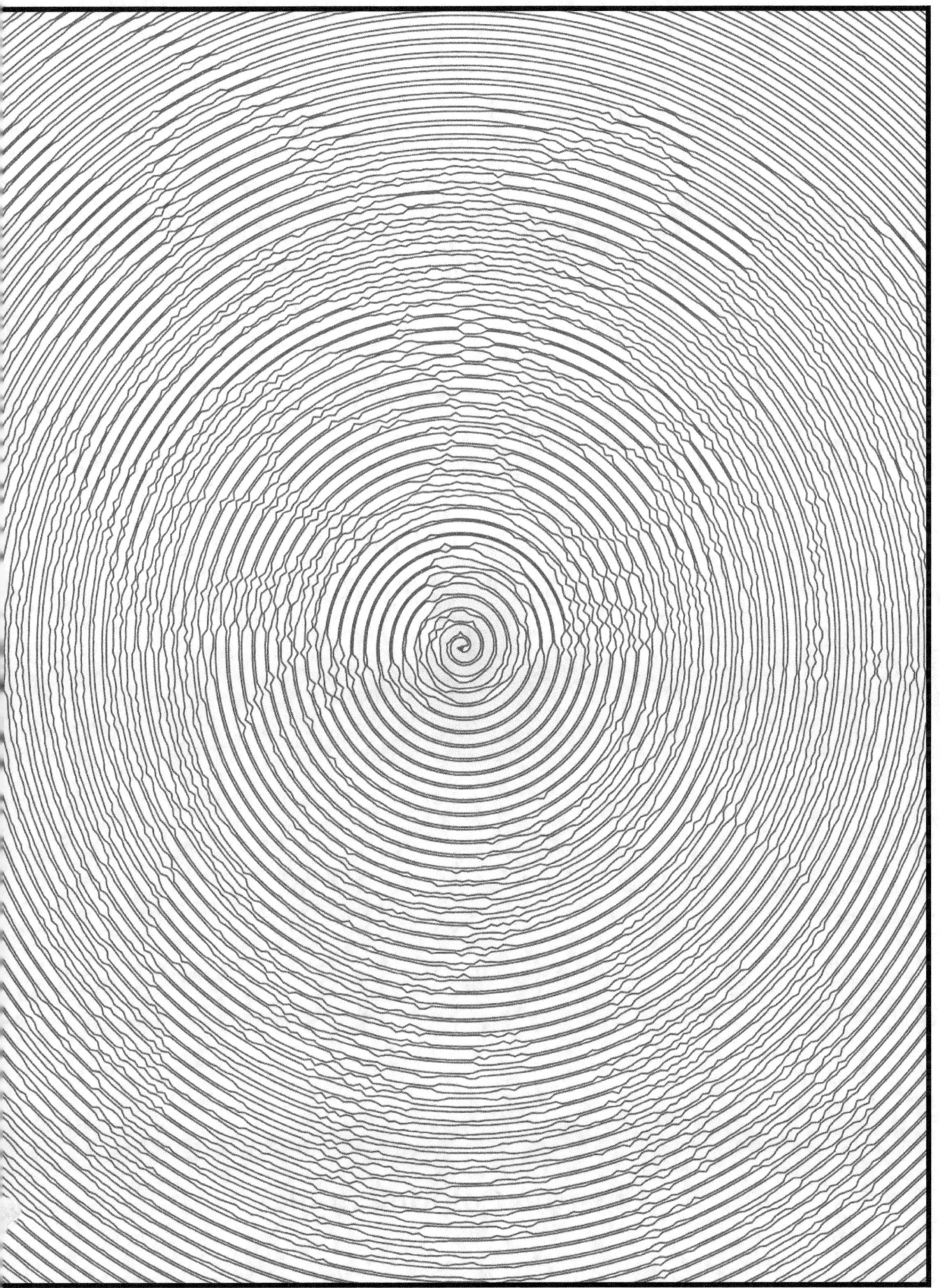

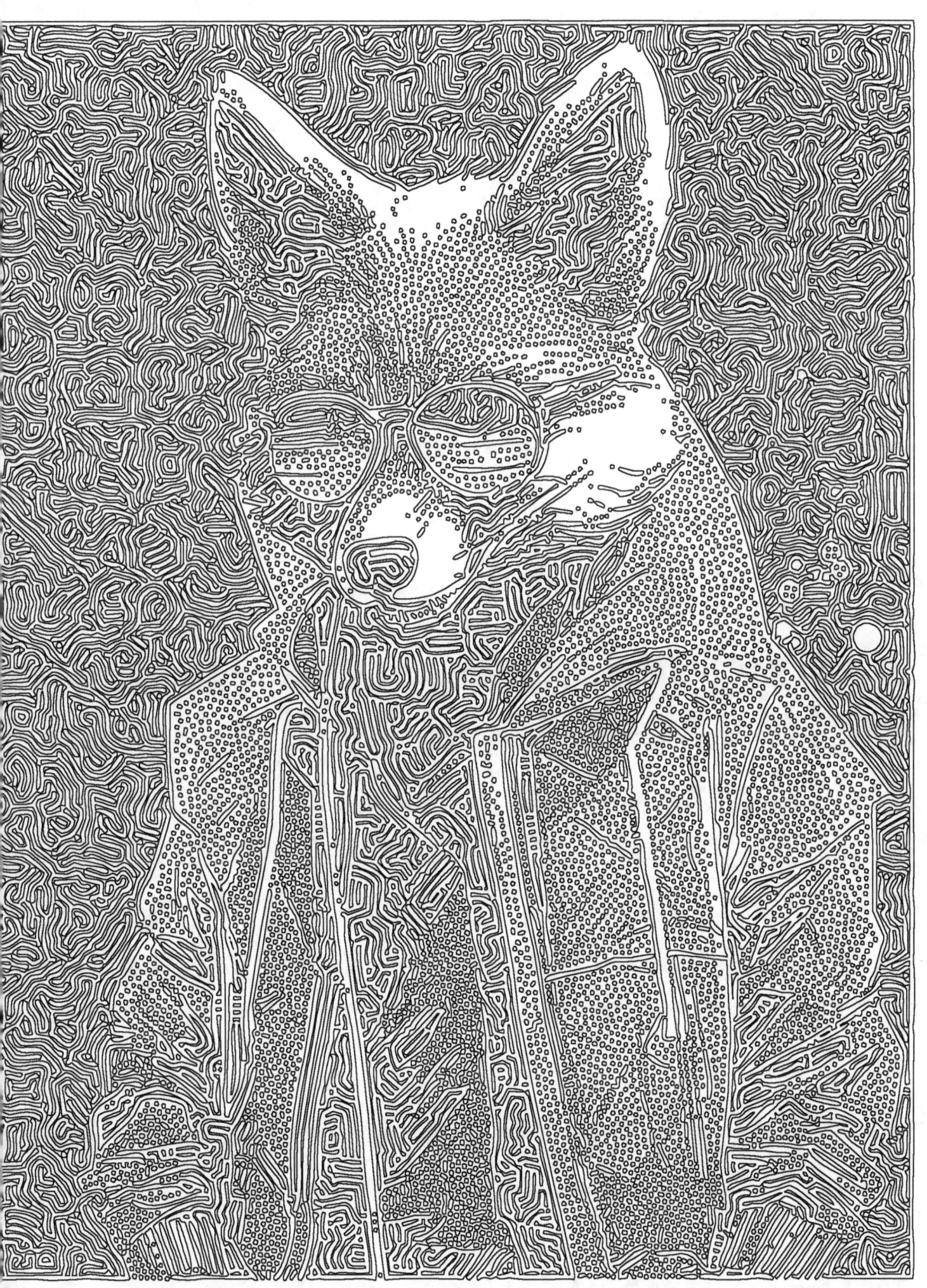

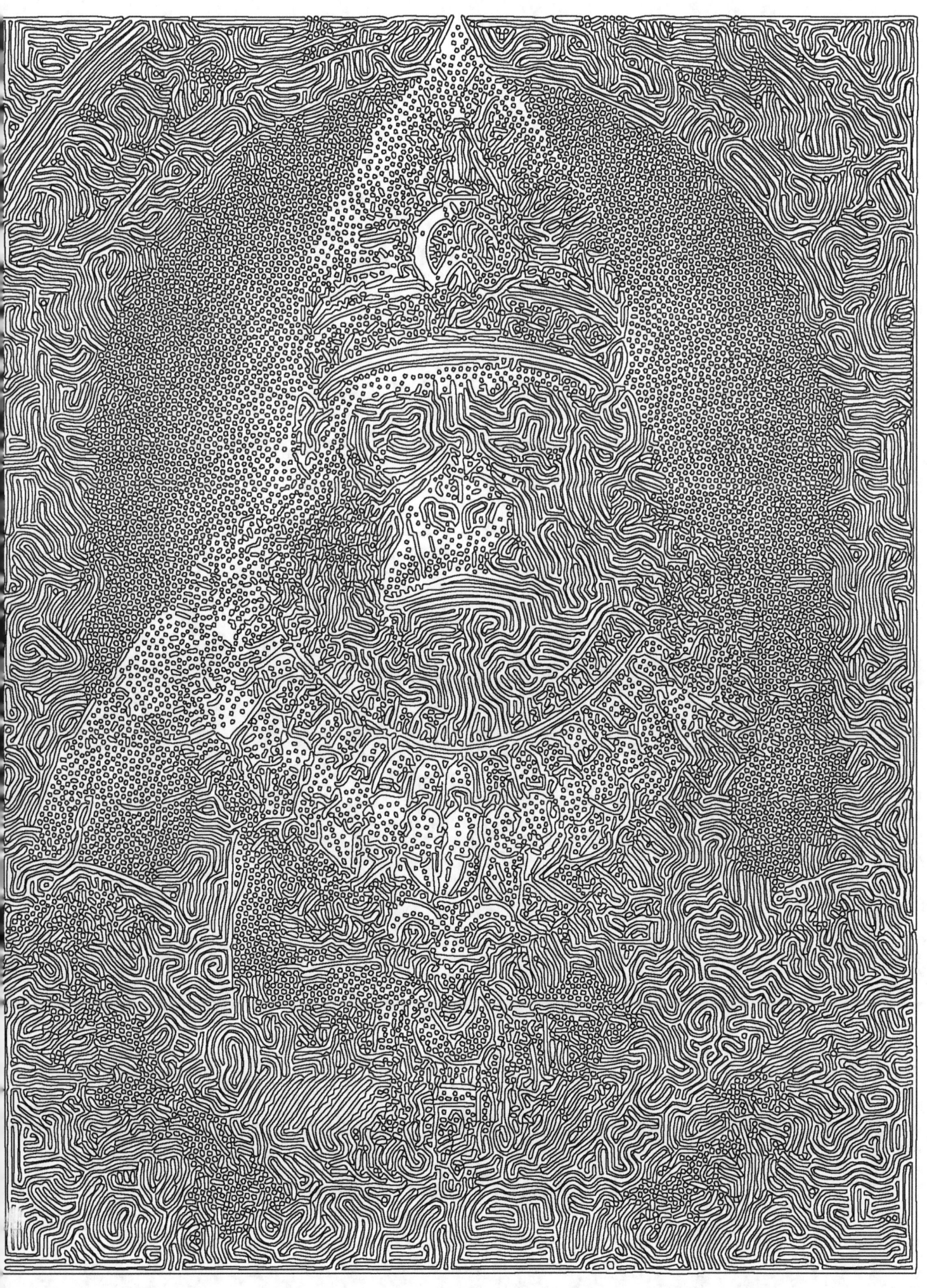

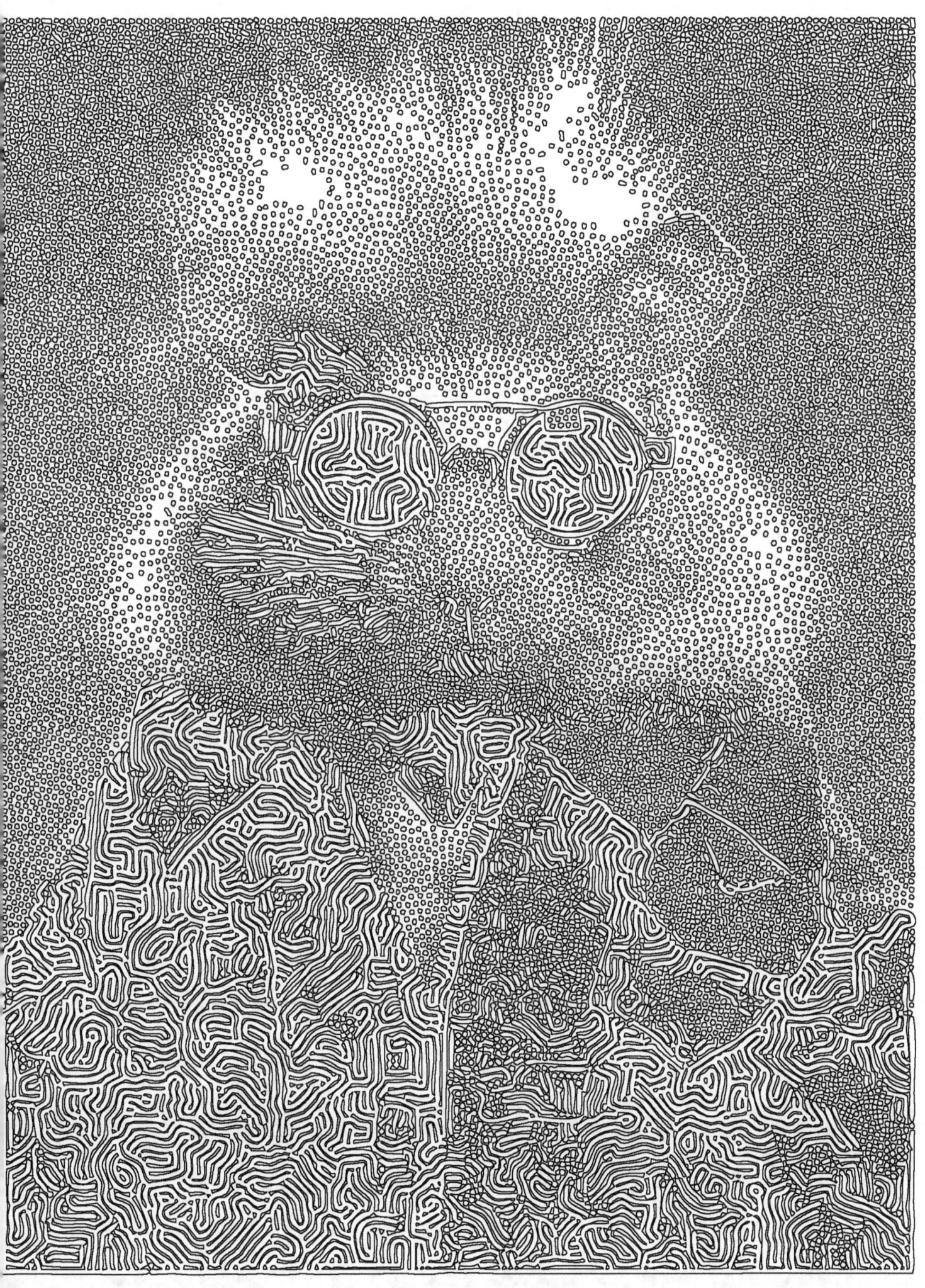

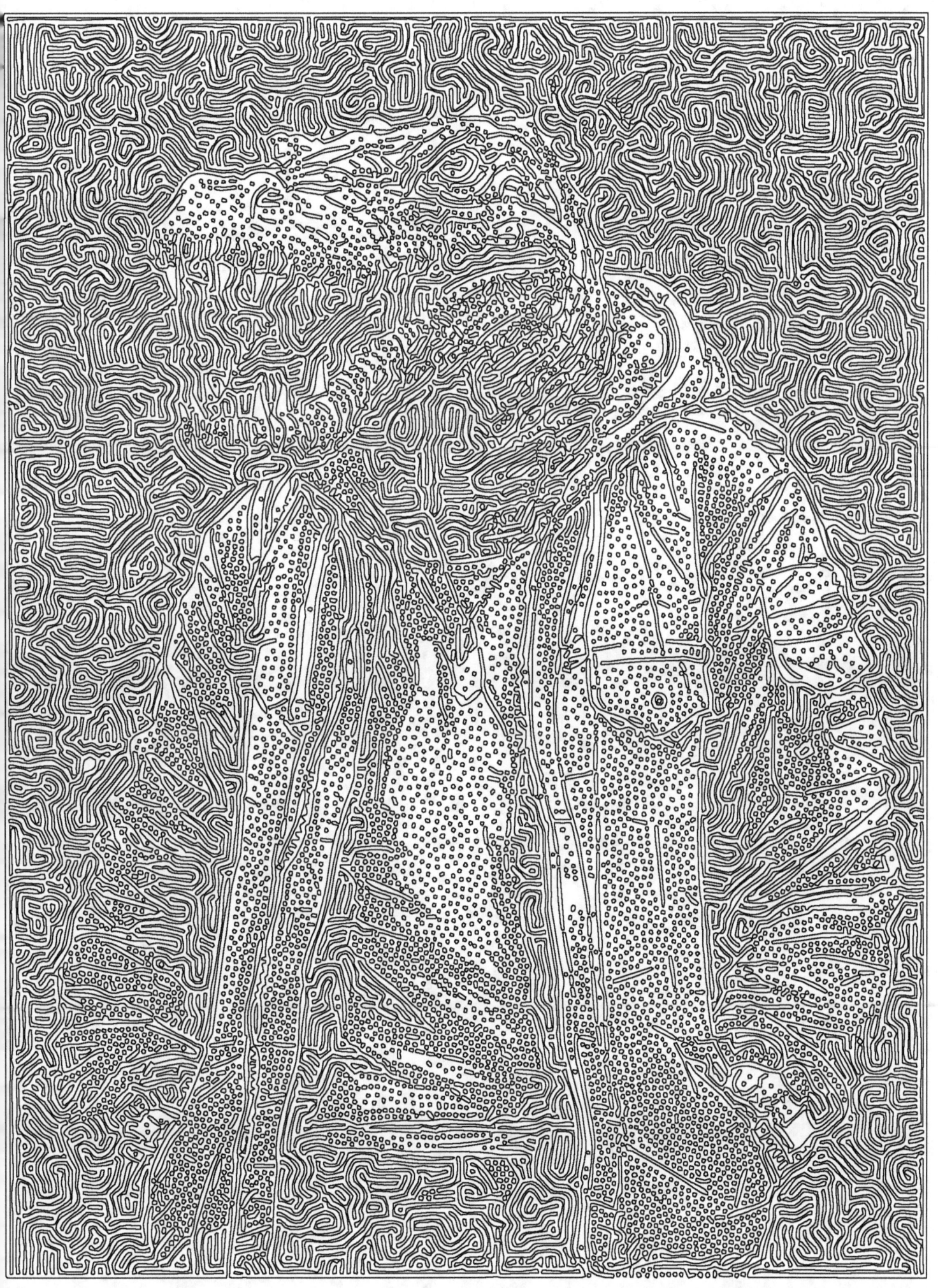

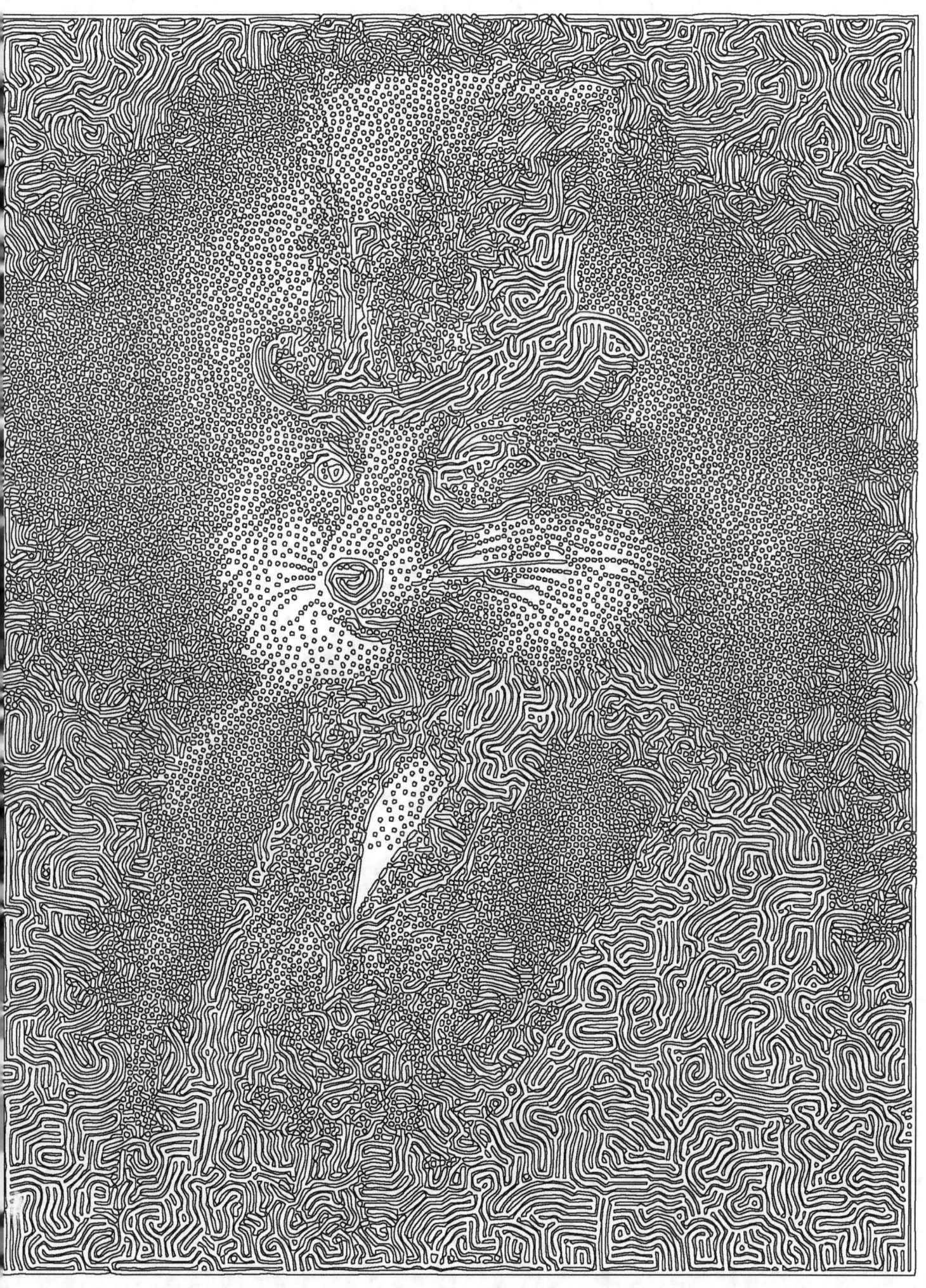

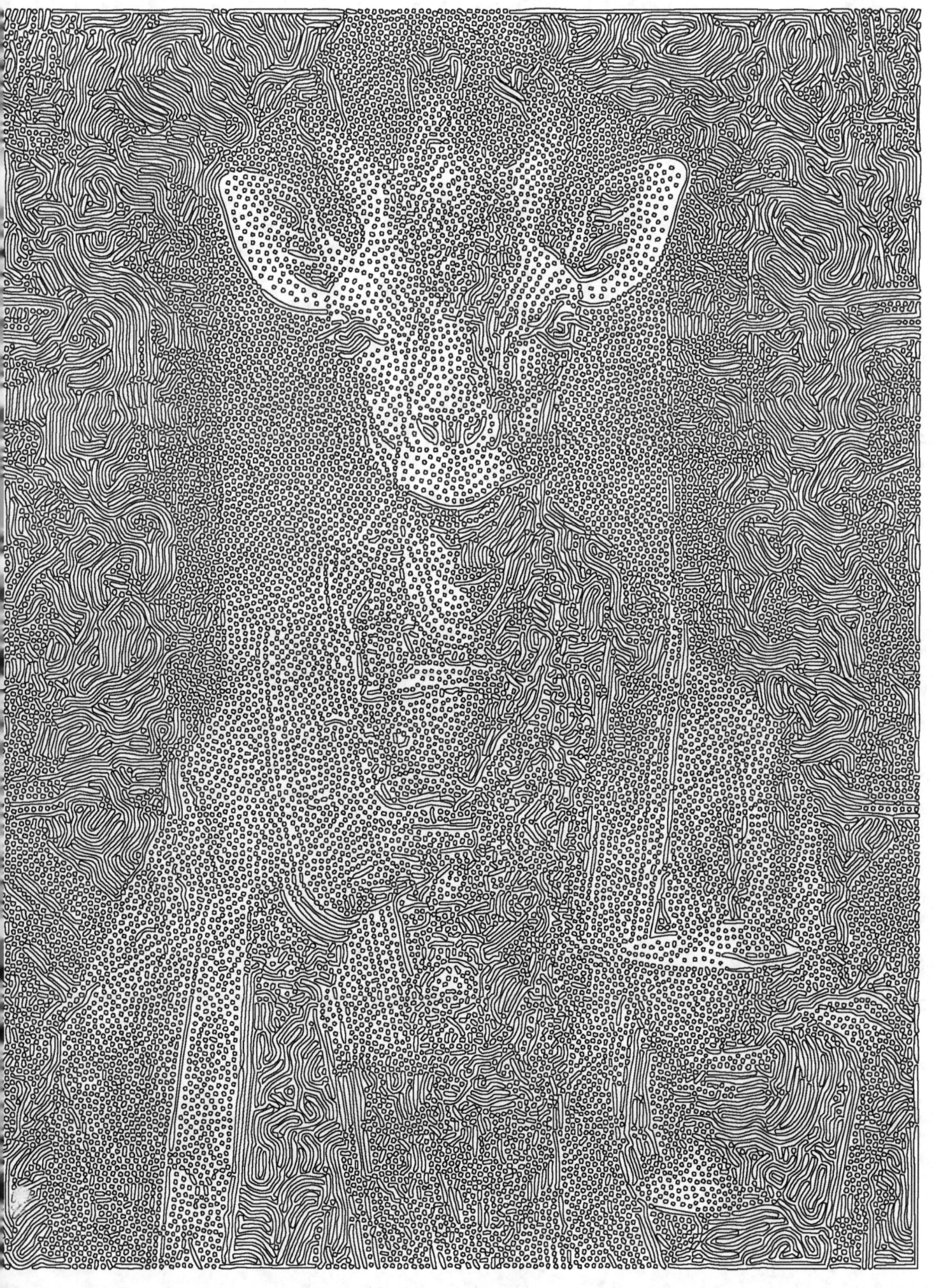

- Lily Ann Coloring Book -

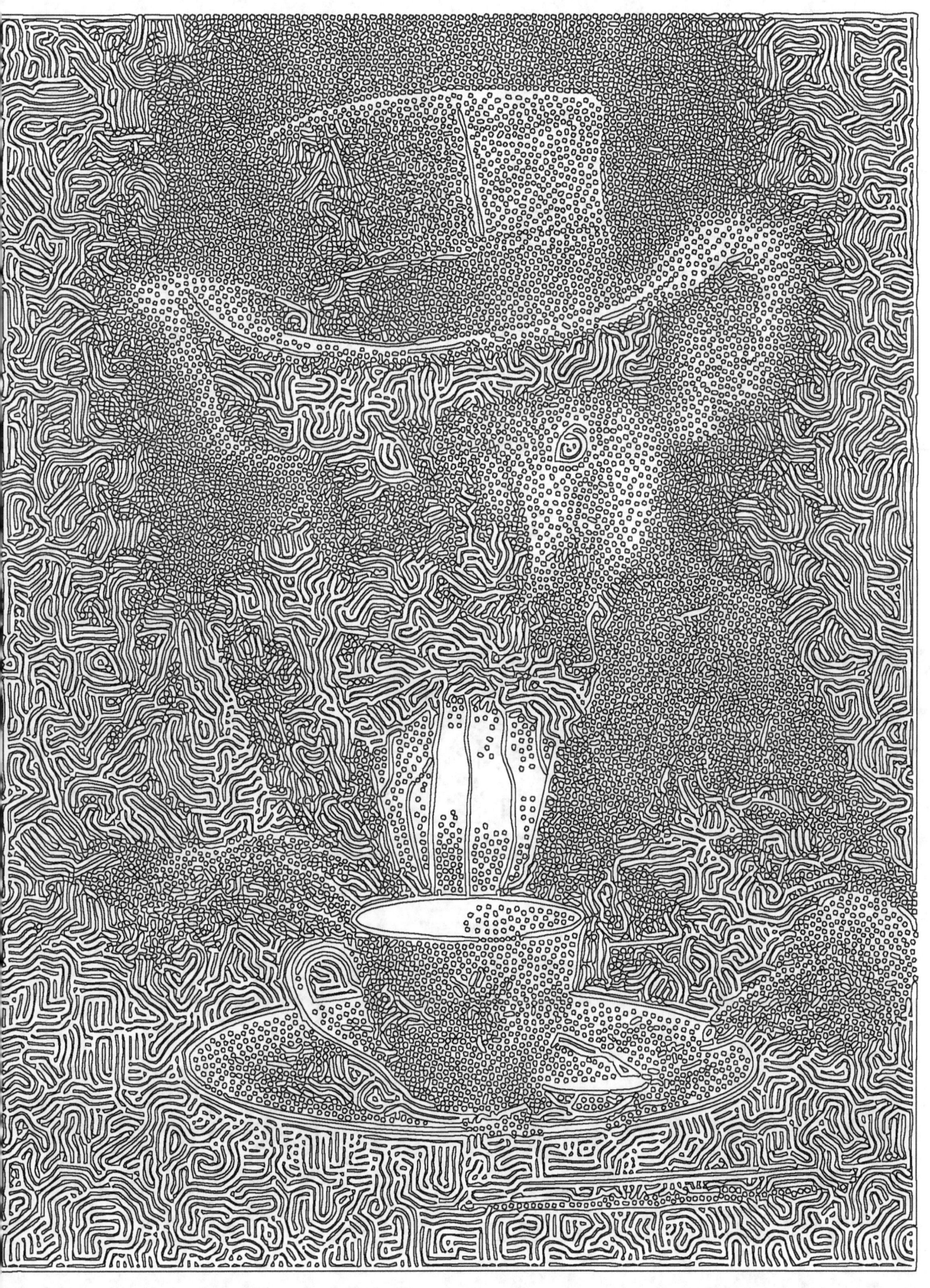

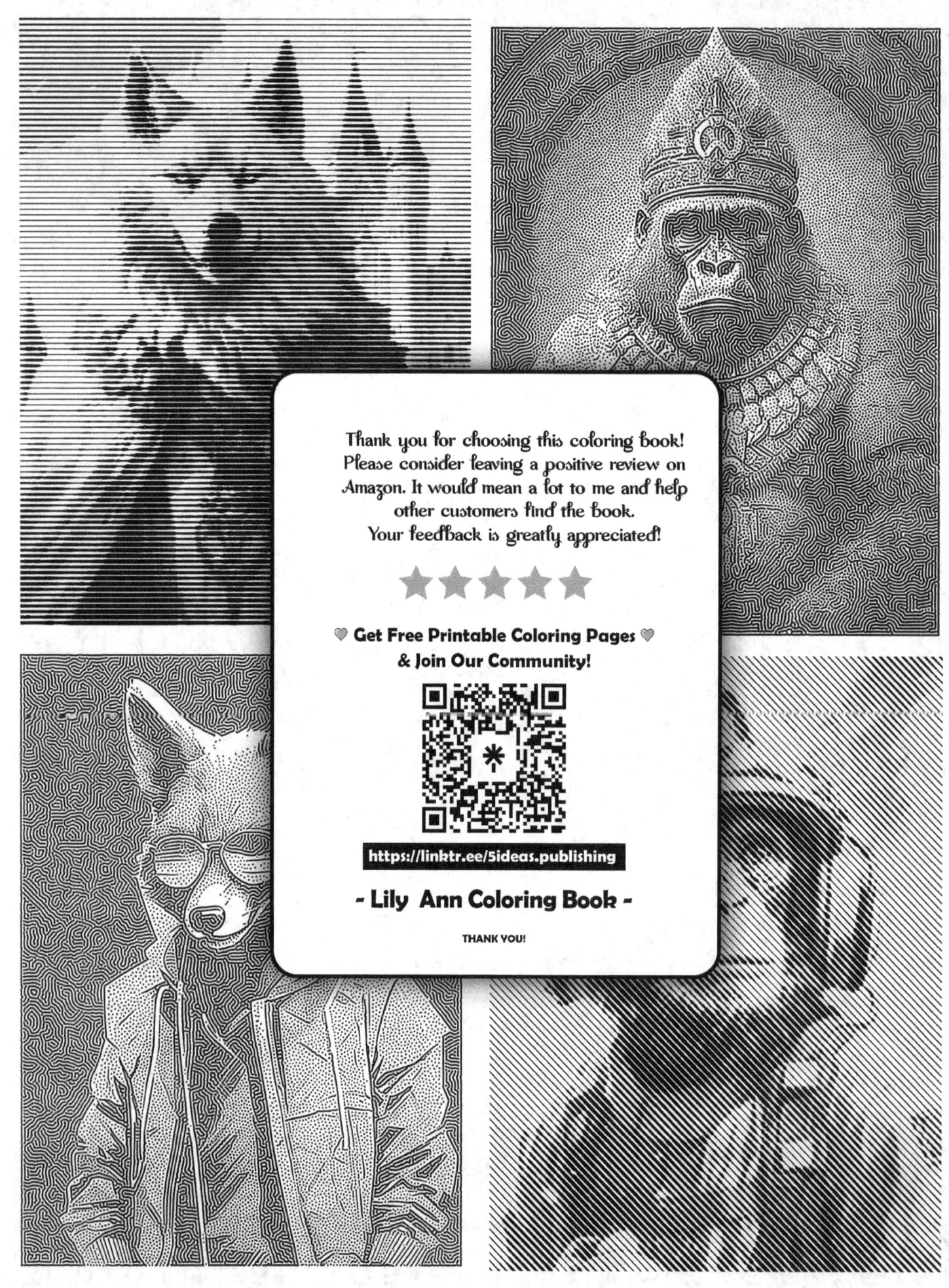

Thank you for choosing this coloring book!
Please consider leaving a positive review on
Amazon. It would mean a lot to me and help
other customers find the book.
Your feedback is greatly appreciated!

★★★★★

🤍 **Get Free Printable Coloring Pages** 🤍
& Join Our Community!

https://linktr.ee/5ideas.publishing

- Lily Ann Coloring Book -

THANK YOU!

THANK YOU FOR CHOOSING US
TRY OUR OTHER COLORING BOOKS ON AMAZON

- Lily Ann Coloring Book -

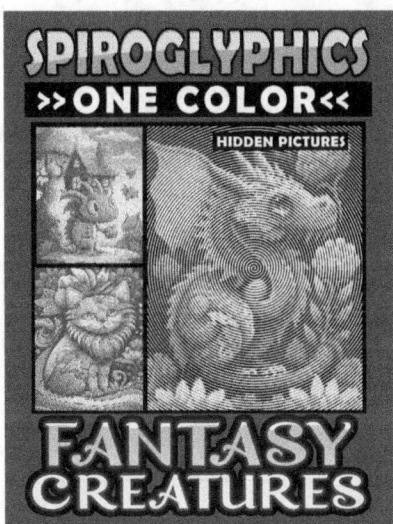

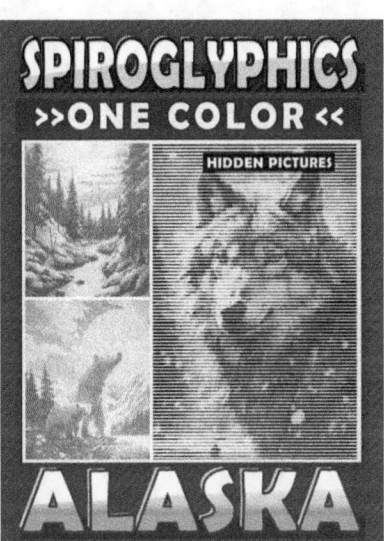

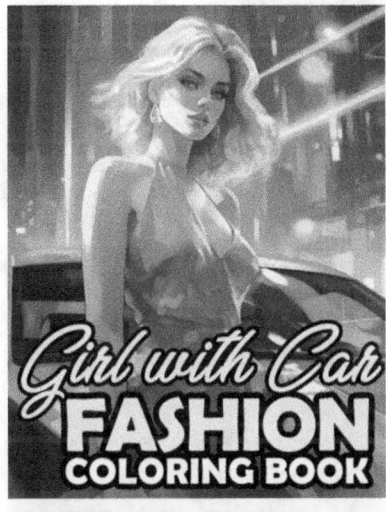

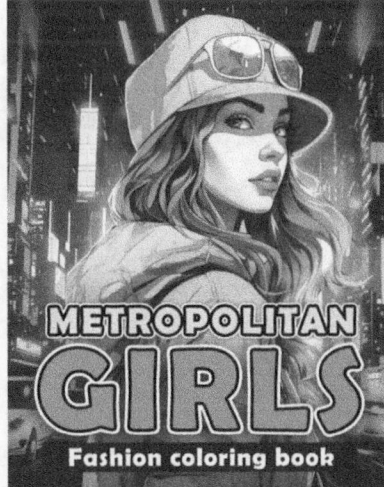

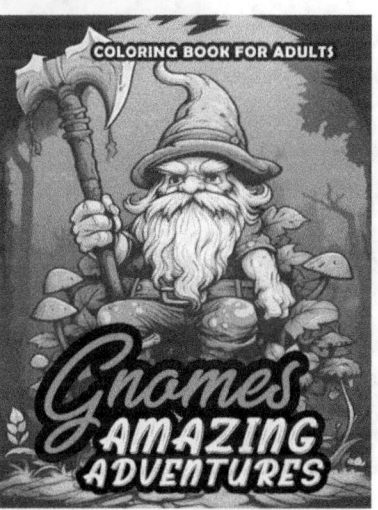

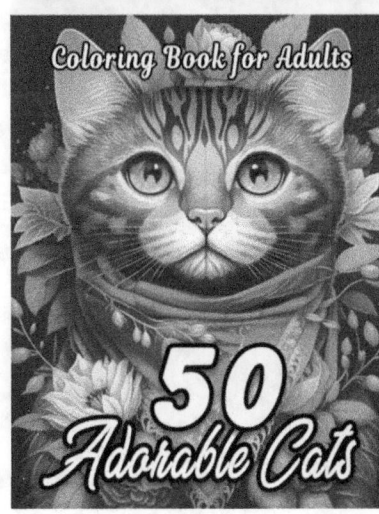

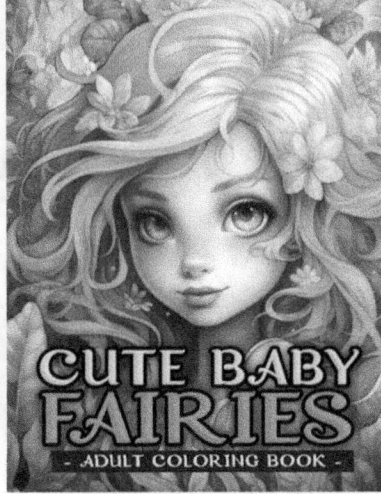

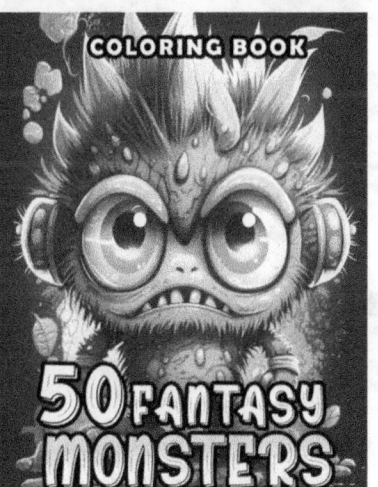